주제별
600단어 따라쓰기

기획 : 와이앤엠 어학연구소

와이 앤 엠

차 례

주제별
600단어 따라쓰기

1. 집 · 가구

apartment
아파트
[əpá:rtmənt
아파-알트먼트]

apartment   apartment

basket
바구니
[bǽskit 배스킷]

basket   basket   basket

bell
종, 초인종
[bel 벨]

bell   bell   bell   bell   bell

bench
긴 의자, 벤치
[bentʃ 벤취]

bench   bench   bench

- I really like my apartment.
- What do you have in your basket?
- Listen! The bell is ringing.
- There are three benches in the park.

나는 우리 아파트가 정말 좋아요.

바구니 안에 뭐가 있어요?

들어봐~ 종이 울리고 있어.

공원에는 벤치가 3개 있다.

4

chair
의자

[tʃɛər 췌어ㄹ]

chair   chair

cup
컵

[kʌp 컵]

cup   cup   cup   cup

curtain
커튼

[kə́ːrtn 커튼]

curtain   curtain   curtain

dish
접시

[diʃ 디쉬]

dish   dish   dish

door
문

[dɔːr 도얼]

door   door   door   door

- There is a cat under the chair.
- I bought this cup for mom.
- I hid behind the curtain.
- I sometimes help mom to wash the dishes.
- I knocked on the door.

의자 밑에 고양이 한 마리가 있어요.
나는 엄마 드리려고 이 컵을 샀어요.
전 커튼 뒤로 숨었어요.
저는 가끔 엄마가 설거지하는 것을 도와드려요.
나는 문을 두드렸어요.

garden
정원

[gáːrdn
가-ㄹ든]

garden   garden   garden

gas
가스

[gæs 개스]

gas   gas   gas   gas   gas

glass
유리, 유리컵

[glæs 글래쓰]

glass   glass   glass   glass

home
집

[hóum 홈]

home   home

kitchen
부엌

[kítʃin 킷췬]

kitchen   kitchen

- There are roses in that garden.   저 정원엔 장미가 있어요.
- We filled the ballon with gas.   우리는 풍선에 가스를 채웠다.
- I drink three glasses of milk everyday.   나는 매일 우유를 세 잔씩 마셔요.
- I have to stay at home today.   나는 오늘 집에 있어야만 해요.
- Refrigerator is in the kitchen.   냉장고는 부엌에 있어요.

6

knife
칼

[naif 나이프]

knife   knife   knife   knife

mirror
거울

[mírəɾ 미뤄-ㄹ]

mirror   mirror   mirror

roof
지붕

[ruːf 루-프]

roof   roof   roof   roof   roof

room
방

[ruːm 루-움]

room   room   room

soap
비누

[soup 쏘웁]

soap   soap   soap   soap

- The knife is dangerous.
- She stands before a mirror all day.
- Our house has a red roof.
- I usually study in my room.
- Wash your hand with soap.

그 칼은 위험해요.

그녀는 하루 종일 거울 앞에 서 있다.

우리집에는 빨간 지붕이 있다.

나는 보통 내 방에서 공부해요.

비누로 손을 깨끗이 씻어라.

sofa
소파

[sóufə 쏘우풔]

sofa   sofa   sofa

spoon
숟가락, 스푼

[spuːn 스푸ㅡㄴ]

spoon   spoon   spoon

stair
계단

[stɛər 스떼어]

stair   stair   stair   stair

telephone
전화

[téləfóun 텔레포운]

telephone telephone

window
창(창문)

[wíndou원도우]

window   window   window

- The cushion is on the sofa.   그 쿠션은 소파 위에 있다.
- I ate my meal with a spoon.   나는 숟가락으로 식사를 했다.
- I went up stairs.   나는 계단을 올랐다.
- He is on the telephone.   그는 통화중이다.
- Please open the window.   창문 좀 열어 주세요.

2. 우리 몸

arm
팔

[aːrm 아-ㄹ암]

arm   arm   arm   arm

back
등, 뒤

[bæk 백]

back   back   back   back

body
몸, 신체

[bádi 바디]

body   body   body

ear
귀

[iər 이얼]

ear   ear   ear   ear   ear   ear

- Tom's arm is long.
- I looked at his back.
- My whole body is aching now.
- Rabbits have long ears.

Tom은 팔이 길어요.

난 그의 등을 보았어요.

지금 온몸이 아파요.

토끼의 귀는 길어요.

eye
눈
[ai 아이]

eye eye eye eye eye

face
얼굴
[feis 페이스]

face face face face

finger
손가락
[fíŋgə𝘳 휭거ㄹ]

finger finger finger

foot
발
[fut 풋]

foot foot foot

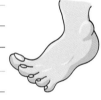

hair
머리카락, 털
[hɛə𝘳 헤얼]

hair hair hair hair hair

- Open your eyes and look around. 눈을 뜨고 주위를 둘러보세요.
- I wash my face everyday. 나는 매일 얼굴을 씻어요(세수해요).
- I touched water with my fingers. 손가락으로 물을 만져보았어요.
- Peter is pushing the box with his foot. Peter는 발로 상자를 밀고 있다.
- Her hair is black and short. 그녀의 머리카락은 검고 짧아.

10

hand
손

[hænd 핸드]

hand   hand   hand   hand

head
머리

[hed 헤드]

head   head   head

heart
마음, 심장

[haːrt하-ㄹ트]

heart   heart   heart   heart

knee
무릎

[niː 니-]

knee   knee   knee

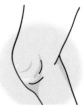

leg
다리

[leg 렉]

leg   leg   leg   leg   leg

- We must wash our hands.
- His head touches the ceiling.
- The doctor is checking my heart.
- I feel pain in my knee.
- I broke my leg three days ago.

손을 꼭 씻어야 해요.
그의 머리는 천장에 닿아요.
의사 선생님이 제 심장을 검사하고 계세요.
무릎이 아파요.
3일전에 다리가 부러졌어요.

lip
입술

[lip 립]

lip   lip   lip   lip   lip   lip

neck
목

[nek 넥]

neck   neck   neck   neck

nose
코

[nouz 노우즈]

nose   nose   nose

tooth
이, 치아

[tu:θ 투-쓰]

tooth   tooth   tooth   tooth

- Her lips turned purple with cold.
- A neck is a part of our body.
- We have a nose.
- Brush your tooth before you go to bed.

추워서 그의 입술이 자줏빛이 되었다.

목은 우리 몸의 한 부분이다.

우리는 하나의 코를 가지고 있다.

자기 전 이를 닦아라.

3. 나 · 그 · 사람

aunt
아주머니, 이모
[ænt 앤트]

aunt　aunt　aunt

baby
아기
[béibi 베이비]

baby　baby　baby

boy
소년
[bɔi 보이]

boy　boy　boy　boy　boy

child
어린이
[tʃaild 촤일드]

child　child　child　child

- I love my aunt Amy.

　저는 Amy 이모가 좋아요.

- The baby girl is my little sister.

　그 여자 아기는 내 여동생이에요.

- Who is that boy?

　저 소년은 누구니?

- The child always wishes to be a man.

　그 어린 아이는 항상 어른이 되기를 바래요.

13

friend
친구

[frend 프뤠ㄴ드]

friend   friend   friend

girl
소녀

[gəːrl 거얼]

girl girl girl girl girl

he
그는, 그가

[hiː 히-]

he he he he he

hers
그녀의 것

[həːrz 허어즈]

hers   hers   hers

I
나는, 내가

[ai 아이]

I I I I I I I I

- I have many friends.   저는 친구가 많아요.
- That girl was wearing a blue skirt.   그 소녀는 파란 치마를 입고 있었다.
- He pointed the girl with a doll.   그는 인형을 가지고 있는 그 소녀를 가르켰어요.
- This comic book is hers.   이 만화책은 그녀의 것이야.
- I'm peter. I'm 10years old.   나는 Peter예요. 10살이죠.

it
그것은

[it 잇]

it it it it it it it it

lady
숙녀, 부인

[léidi 레이디]

lady lady lady lady lady

man
남자

[mæn 맨]

man man man man

mine
나의 것

[máin 마인]

mine mine mine mine

people
사람들, 국민

[píːpl 피-쁠]

people people people

- It is your dog.
- The lady over there is my aunt.
- The man is my father.
- The pen is mine.
- People like flowers.

그것은 당신의 강아지예요.
저기 있는 숙녀분은 우리 고모예요.
그 남자는 나의 아버지예요.
그 펜은 내거야.
사람들은 꽃을 좋아해요.

15

she
그녀는, 그녀가

[ʃiː 쉬]

she she she she

that
저것, 그것

[ðæt 댓]

that that that that

the
그

[ðə/ði 더/디]

the the the the the the

there
거기에

[ðɛər 데얼]

there there there there

they
그들은

[ðei 데이]

they they they

- She is really beautiful.
- Look at that! That is big!
- The girl is my sister.
- Look over there.
- They are going to school.

그녀는 정말 아름다워요.
이 사과들은 빨갛다.
그 소녀는 내 여동생입니다.
저기 좀 봐.
그들은 학교에 가고 있어요.

this 이것 [ðis 디쓰]	this this this this this this
we 우리, 저희가 [wiː 위-]	we we we we we
you 너, 당신 [juː 유-]	you you you you 
yours 너의 것 [juərz 유어즈]	yours yours yours yours

- How about this shirt?　　이 셔츠는 어때요?
- We go to school at 8 o'clock.　　우리는 8시에 등교한다.
- You look so pretty.　　너는 굉장히 예쁘다(너는 참 예쁘구나).
- Yours is beautiful.　　너의 것은 예쁘다.

4. 가족

birthday
생일
[bə́ːrθdèi 벌쓰데이]

birthday   birthday

cousin
사촌, 친척
[kʌ́zn 커즌]

cousin   cousin   cousin

parent
부모님
[pɛ́ərənt 페어뤄ㄴ트]

parent   parent   parent

son
아들
[sɔn 썬]

son   son   son   son   son

- When is your birthday?   네 생일이 언제니?
- This is my cousin, Mike.   애는 내 사촌 Mike야.
- My parents are very nice.   나의 부모님은 매우 좋으신 분이예요.
- He is my son.   그는 나의 아들이다.

5. 음식 · 과일 · 식사

butter
버터

[bʌ́tər 버러ㄹ]

butter butter butter butter

breakfast
아침식사

[brékfəst
브뤼ㄱ풔스트]

breakfast   breakfast

bread
빵

[bred 브레드]

bread bread bread

cake
케이크

[keik 케이크]

cake   cake   cake   cake

- There are bread and butter.   빵과 버터가 있어요.
- I ate bread and milk for breakfast.   나는 아침으로 빵과 우유를 먹었다.
- Tom, would like some bread?   Tom, 빵 좀 먹을래?
- She gave me a piece of cake.   그녀는 나에게 케이크 한 조각을 주었다.

candy
사탕
[kǽndi 캔디]

candy candy candy

cheese
치즈
[tʃiːz 취-즈]

cheese cheese cheese

corn
옥수수
[kɔːrn 콘]

corn corn corn corn corn

cream
크림
[kriːm 크뤼-임]

cream cream cream

cucumber
오이
[kjúːkʌmbər 큐컴벌]

cucumber cucumber

- Andy gave me a candy.
- Mice are eating cheese.
- Do you like corn?
- Put two spoons of cream.
- A cucumber is long and green.

Andy가 나에게 사탕을 주었어요.
쥐들이 치즈를 먹고 있어요.
옥수수 좋아하세요?
크림 두 스푼을 넣으세요.
오이는 길고 녹색이다.

dinner
저녁 식사

[dínər 디널]

dinner　dinner　dinner

egg
달걀

[eg 엑]

egg　egg　egg　egg

food
음식

[fuːd 푸-드]

food　food　food　food

fruit
과일

[fruːt 푸룻-트]

fruit　fruit　fruit　fruit　fruit

hamburger
햄버거

[hǽmbəːrgər 햄버거]

hamburger　hamburger

- I had dinner with my friend, Tony.
- Chickens lay an egg each morning.
- What is your favorite food?
- What is your favorite fruit?
- Are you eating hamburger again?

나는 친구 Tony와 저녁을 먹었어요.
닭은 매일 아침 달걀을 한 개씩 낳아요.
좋아하는 음식은 무엇인가요?
좋아하는 과일이 무엇인가요?
너 햄버거 또 먹는거야?

21

Juice
주스

[dʒúːs 쥬-스]

juice   juice   juice

meat
고기

[miː t 미-잇트]

meat   meat   meat   meat

pear
(과일)배

[pɛər 페얼]

pear   pear   pear   pear

rice
쌀, 밥

[rais 롸이스]

rice   rice   rice   rice   rice

salad
샐러드

[sǽləd 쌜러드]

salad   salad   salad

- Would you like some juice?
- We will have meat for dinner.
- This pear is sweet.
- Korean usually eat rice.
- I ate some salad and chicken.

주스 좀 드실래요?
우리는 저녁식사로 고기를 먹을 거야.
이 배는 달다.
한국 사람들은 보통 밥을 먹는다.
나는 샐러드와 치킨을 먹었다.

salt
소금
[sɔːlt 써-얼트]

salt salt salt salt salt

strawberry
딸기
[strɔ́ːbéri,
스뜨뤄-베뤼]

strawberry

supper
저녁식사
[sʌ́pər 써퍼얼]

supper supper supper

tomato
토마토
[təméitou
터메이토]

tomato tomato tomato

- Could you pass me the salt, please. 소금 좀 건내 주시겠어요?
- I like strawberry. 나는 딸기를 좋아해요.
- Supper is the last meal of the day. 저녁식사는 하루의 마지막 식사이다.
- My mother likes tomato juice. 엄마는 토마토주스를 좋아하세요.

6. 옷 · 액세서리

button
단추, 버튼
[bʌ́tn 버튼]

button   button   button

cap
모자
[kæp 캡]

cap   cap   cap   cap

clothes
옷
[klouðz클로우즈]

clothes   clothes   clothes

coat
외투
[kout 코웃]

coat   coat   coat   coat   coat

- The baby is touching the buttons.
- Mom bought me this cap.
- I'm making clothes for my cat.
- My grandfather bought me a blue coat.

아기가 단추를 만지고 있어요.

엄마가 이 모자를 사주셨어요.

지금 제 고양이에게 입힐 옷을 만들고 있어요.

할아버지께서 파란색 코트를 사주셨어요.

dress
의복

[dres 드뢰스]

dress dress dress

pants
바지

[pænts 팬츠]

pants pants pants pants

pocket
호주머니

[pákit 파킷]

pocket pocket pocket

ring
반지

[riŋ 륑]

ring ring ring

shirt
셔츠

[ʃəːrt 셔-ㄹ츠]

shirt shirt shirt shirt

- I want to wear the pink dress.
- Tom always wear same pants.
- She put her hand in her pockets.
- He gave me a ring.
- I bought this shirt last year.

분홍색 드레스(옷)를 입고 싶어요.
탐은 항상 같은 바지를 입어.
그녀는 주머니에 손을 넣었어요.
그가 나에게 반지를 주었어요.
작년에 이 셔츠를 샀어요.

shoe
신, 구두

[ʃuː 슈-]

shoe　shoe　shoe　shoe

skirt
스커트

[skəːrt 스꺼얼트]

skirt　skirt　skirt

sweater
스웨터

[swétər 스웨터]

sweater sweater sweater

tie
넥타이

[tai 타이]

tie　tie　tie　tie　tie

umbrella
우산

[ʌmbrélə 엄브뤌러]

umbrella　umbrella

- My father bought a pair of shoes for me.
- That skirt looks cool.
- This sweater is warm.
- I must wear a tie tonight.
- He has an umbrella in his hand.

아빠가 저에게 신발(한켤레)을 사주셨어요.
저 치마 멋져보여.
이 스웨터는 따뜻하다.
저는 오늘 꼭 넥타이를 매야해요.
그의 손에 우산이 있다(그는 우산을 들고 있어요).

7. 스포츠 · 취미

art
미술, 예술
[ɑːrt 알트]

art art art art art art

club
클럽, 동호회
[klʌb 클럽]

club club club club club

exercise
운동, 연습
[éksərsáiz 엑썰싸이즈]

exercise exercise exercise

dance
춤, 춤추다
[dæns 댄스]

dance dance dance

- My favorite subject is art.   내가 가장 좋아하는 과목은 미술이다.
- He is my club friend.   그는 내 동호회 친구야.
- It's important to exercise everyday.   매일 운동하는 것은 중요해요.
- I like to dance.   저는 춤추는 걸 좋아해요.

drum
북, 드럼

[drʌm 드럼]

drum　drum　drum　drum

film
필름, 영화

[film 필름]

film　film　film　film

game
게임

[geim 게임]

game　game　game

movie
영화

[múːvi 무-뷔]

movie　movie　movie

music
음악

[mjúːzik 뮤-직]

music music music

- Peter is playing the drum.
- My parents like to go to see a film.
- I like to play computer games.
- I went to the movie with my friends.
- I like listening to music.

Peter가 드럼을 치고 있어요.
부모님은 영화보는 것을 좋아하세요.
컴퓨터 게임 하는 거 좋아해요.
나는 친구들과 영화를 보러 갔다.
나는 음악 듣는 것을 좋아한다.

sing
노래, 노래하다

[siŋ 씽]

sing sing sing sing sing

skate
스케이트

[skeit 스케잇-ㅌ]

skate skate skate skate

soccer
축구

[sάkər 싸커ㄹ]

soccer soccer soccer

song
노래

[sɔːŋ 쏭]

song song song song

sport
스포츠

[spɔːrt 스포-올트]

sport sport sport sport

- My hobby is to sing songs.
- Let's go skating!
- I played soccer with my friends.
- I sang a song for my parents.
- Soccer is a popular sport in korea.

내 취미는 노래 부르는 것이다.
스케이트 타러가자!
나는 친구들과 축구를 했어요.
나는 부모님을 위해 노래를 불렀어요.
한국에서 축구는 인기가 좋다.

29

swim
수영하다, 수영

[swim 스윔]

swim swim swim

swing
그네

[swiŋ 스윙]

swing swing swing swing

team
팀

[ti:m 팀]

team team team team

tennis
테니스

[ténis 테니스]

tennis tennis tennis

video
비디오

[vídióú
브이디오]

video video video

- We went swimming last Sunday.
- There are two boys on the swing.
- His team won the game.
- She played tennis with her friend.
- How often do you rent video tapes?

지난 일요일 우리는 수영하러 갔다.
그네에 남자아이 둘이 타고 있다.
그의 팀이 게임에서 이겼다.
그녀는 친구와 함께 테니스를 쳤다.
당신은 얼마나 자주 비디오 테이프를 빌려요?

8. 학생 · 학용품

bag
가방, 봉지
[bæg 백]

bag   bag   bag   bag

board
판자, 게시판
[bɔːrd 보-ㄹ드]

board board board board

camp
캠프
[kæmp 캠프]

camp   camp   camp   camp

chalk
분필
[tʃɔːk 초어크]

chalk chalk chalk chalk

- This is my schoolbag.　　　　이건 제 책가방이예요.
- What's this new board for?　이 새 게시판은 어디에 쓸 거죠?
- Let's go camping.　　　　　　캠핑하러 가자.
- Let's buy blackboard and chalk.　칠판과 분필을 삽시다.

class
수업, 학급

[klæs 클래스]

class   class   class

computer
컴퓨터

[kəmpjúːtər
컴퓨-러ㄹ]

computer   computer

crayon
크레용

[kréiən
크래이언]

crayon   crayon   crayon

desk
책상

[desk 데스크]

desk   desk   desk   desk

eraser
지우개

[iréisəʌ̀ər
이뢰이줘ㄹ]

eraser eraser eraser

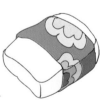

- It's time to finish the class.
- There are three compurters on the desk.
- I like to draw lines using crayons.
- There is a pencil on the desk.
- Tom, can I borrow your eraser?

수업을 끝낼 시간이에요.
책상 위에 컴퓨터가 3대 있어요.
크레용으로 선긋는 것을 좋아해요.
책상 위에 연필 한 자루가 있어요.
Tom, 지우개 좀 빌려줄래?

learn
배우다
[ləːrn 러-ㄹ언]

learn   learn   learn   learn

lesson
수업
[lésn 렛쓴]

lesson   lesson   lesson

library
도서관
[láibreri
라이브뢰뤼]

library   library   library

paper
종이
[péipər페이펄]

paper   paper   paper

pin
핀
[pin 핀]

pin   pin   pin   pin   pin   pin

- I want to learn English.
- I have no lesson today.
- Mom and I often go to a library.
- I need a sheet of paper.
- Please, lend me a safety pin.

전 영어를 배우고 싶어요.
오늘은 수업이 하나도 없어요.
엄마랑 저는 가끔 도서관에 가요.
종이 한 장이 필요하다.
안전핀 좀 빌려 주시겠어요.

school
학교, 수업

[sku:l 스꾸-울]

school school school

student
학생

[stjú:dənt
스츄-던트]

student   student   student

study
공부하다

[stʌ́di 스떠디]

study   study   study   study

table
테이블

[téibl 테이블]

table   table   table

test
시험, 검사

[test 테스트]

test   test   test   test   test

- After school, I came back home.
- How many students are there?
- At school, I study English.
- There are two books on the table.
- I had a test last Friday.

수업이 끝난 후, 나는 집으로 돌아 왔어요.
학생이 몇 명 있죠?
학교에서, 나는 영어를 공부한다.
테이블 위에 책이 2권 있다.
지난 금요일에 나는 시험을 봤다.

9. 색

black
검은 색
[blæk 블랙]

black   black   black   black

blue
파란색
[blu: 블루-]

blue   blue   blue

brown
갈색, 갈색의
[braun 브롸운]

brown   brown   brown

color
색깔
[kʌlər 컬러ㄹ]

color   color   color   color

- The prince has black hair.　　　왕자 머리카락은 검은색이에요.
- Jessica has blue eyes.　　　Jessica의 눈은 파란색이예요.
- My teacher wears brown jacket.　　　선생님은 갈색 자켓을 입고 계시다.
- What is your favorite color?　　　가장 좋아하는 색이 뭐야?

gray
회색, 회색의

[grei 그뢰이]

gray   gray   gray   gray

pink
분홍

[piŋk 핑크]

pink   pink   pink   pink

red
빨간색, 붉은

[red 뢰드]

red red red red red red

white
흰, 흰빛

[hwait 와이트]

white white white white

yellow
노랑

[jélou 옐로–]

yellow   yellow

- I like this gray sweater.
- I like the pink.
- She was red with shame.
- We can see the white color in the dark.
- The banana is yellow.

나는 이 회색 스웨터가 좋아.
나는 분홍색을 좋아해요.
그녀는 부끄러워서 얼굴이 빨개졌다.
우리는 어둠 속에서 흰색을 볼 수 있다.
바나나는 노랑색이다.

10. 직업 · 삶

captain
선장, 우두머리
[kǽptin 캡틴]

captain   captain   captain

cook
요리사
[kúk 쿡]

cook   cook   cook

doctor
의사
[dáktər닥터ㄹ]

doctor doctor doctor

job
일, 직업
[dʒab 좝]

job job job job job job

- Mr. Han is the captain of the soccer team.
- My mom is a great cook.
- I would like to be a doctor.
- "What's her job?"

한선생님은 그 축구팀의 주장이에요.

우리 엄마는 훌륭한 요리사다.

나는 의사가 되고 싶어요.

그녀의 직업은 무엇인가요?

nurse
간호사

[nəːrs 널쓰]

nurse nurse nurse

pilot
조종사

[páilət 파일럿]

pilot pilot pilot pilot pilot

police
경찰

[pəlíːs 펄리-스]

police police police

course
진로, 과정

[kɔːrs 코-ㄹ스]

course course course

god
하느님

[gad 가드]

god god god god

- She is a nurse.
- I want to be a pilot.
- Police caught a thief.
- The full course is finished now.
- Oh, God.

그녀는 간호사이다.
나는 조종사가 되고 싶어요.
경찰이 도둑을 잡았어요.
전 과정이 이제 끝났어요.
오, 신이시여.

group
무리, 모임, 떼

[gruːp 구루웁]

group group group

king
왕

[kiŋ 킹]

king king king king

letter
편지

[létər 레러-ㄹ]

letter letter letter letter

life
생명, 생활

[laif 라이프]

life life life life life

live
살다

[liv 리브]

live live live live live

- Each group has its flag.   각 그룹마다 깃발이 있어요.
- The lion is the king of animals.   사자는 동물의 왕이에요.
- I send a letter to my friend Min-su.   나는 친구 민수에게 편지를 보내요.
- Thank you for saving my life.   제 생명을 구해주셔서 감사해요.
- Where do you live?   사시는 곳이 어디예요?

luck
행운

[lɔk 럭]

luck　luck　luck　luck　luck

mail
우편

[meil 메일]

mail　　mail　　mail

marry
결혼하다

[mǽri 매뤼]

marry　marry　marry　marry

party
파티, 모임

[pάːrti 파-ㄹ리]

party　party　party　party

peace
평화

[piːs 피-스]

peace　　peace　　peace

- Good luck!　　　　　　　　　　　　행운을 빌어요.
- I send a letter by mail.　　　　　　나는 편지를 우편으로 보낸다.
- He will marry a woderful woman.　그는 멋진 여성과 결혼할 것이다.
- Can you come to my party?　　　　내 파티에 올래?
- I want the world peace.　　　　　　나는 세계 평화를 원한다.

sleep
잠자다
[sliːp 슬리-입]

sleep sleep sleep sleep

town
마을
[táun 타운]

town town town town

village
마을, 촌락
[vílidʒ 빌리쥐]

village village village

welcome
환영하다
[wélkəm 웰컴]

welcome welcome

- I went to sleep at 9 o'clock.
- I live in town.
- The farmer lives in the village.
- Welcome to Korea!

나는 9시에 잤어요.

나는 마을에 살아요.

그 농부는 마을에 살아요.

한국에 오신 걸 환영합니다!

11. 탈것

airplane 비행기 [ɛ́ərplén 에얼플레인]	airplane airplane airplane
ambulance 구급차 [ǽmb앰뷸런스]	ambulance ambulance
bicycle 자전거 [báisikəl바이시클]	bicycle bicycle 
boat 보트, 작은배 [bout 보웃트]	boat boat boat boat

- I go to Busan by airplane.　　　　　　나는 부산에 비행기로 간다.
- The ambulance is arriving.　　　　　 구급차가 도착하고 있다.
- Can you ride a bicycle?　　　　　　　자전거를 탈 수 있나요?
- My uncle has a big boat.　　　　　　삼촌은 큰 보트를 가지고 계신다.

ship
배

[ʃip 쉽]

ship ship ship ship

sled
썰매

[sled 슬레드]

sled sled sled sled sled

subway
지하철

[sʌ́bwéi
써브웨이]

subway subway

train
기차

[trein 츄뢰인]

train train train

truck
트럭

[trʌk 츄럭]

truck truck truck truck

- Look at that ship!
- In winter, we sled.
- We went to In-cheon by subway.
- I will travel by train.
- The truck is big.

저 배를 봐요!
겨울에 우리는 썰매를 탄다.
우리는 지하철로 인천에 갔다.
나는 기차로 여행할 거예요.
저 트럭은 크다.

airport
공항

[ɛ́ərpɔ̀ːrt 에어포-르트]

airport airport airport

bank
은행

[bæŋk 뱅크]

bank   bank   bank   bank

bridge
다리

[bridʒ 브릿쥐]

bridge   bridge

capital
수도, 서울

[kǽpitl 캐피틀]

capital   capital   capital

church
교회

[tʃəːtʃ 춰-ㄹ취]

church   church

- Is there a bus to airport?
- My father works for that bank.
- We walked across the bridge.
- Seoul is the capital of Korea.
- I go to church on Sundays.

공항으로 가는 버스가 있어요?
우리 아빠는 저 은행에서 일하셔요.
우리는 걸어서 다리를 건넜어요.
서울은 대한민국의 수도예요.
저는 일요일마다 교회에 가요.

city
도시
[síti 씨티]

city city city city city city

floor
바닥, 층
[flɔːr 플로-월]

floor floor floor floor

gate
문, 출입구
[geit 게잇트]

gate gate gate gate

hospital
병원
[háspitl 하스피틀]

hospital hospital hospital

hotel
호텔
[houtél 호텔]

hotel hotel hotel hotel

- There are lots of people in the city.
- The book store is on the third floor.
- There is a dog at the gate.
- Ted is in the hospital.
- How about staying in a hotel?

이 도시에는 사람들이 아주 많아요.
그 서점은 3층에 있어요.
문 앞에 개가 한 마리 있어요.
Ted는 병원에 입원해 있어요.
호텔에 묵는 건 어때요?

office
사무실

[ɔ́:fis 어-퓌스]

office office office

picnic
소풍

[píknik 피크닉]

picnic picnic picnic

place
장소, 곳

[pleis 플레이스]

place place place place

restaurant
레스토랑

[réstərənt 뢰스토뢴트드]

restaurant restaurant

road
길, 도로

[roud 로우드]

road road road

- He works hard in his office.
- We went on a picnic last weekend.
- The place is very nice.
- We had a dinner at restaurant.
- The road is narrow.

그는 그의 사무실에서 열심히 일한다.
우리는 지난 주말에 소풍을 갔다.
그 장소는 매우 멋져.
우리는 레스토랑에서 저녁을 먹었어요.
그 도로는 좁아요.

seat
자리, 좌석

[siːt 씨-잇트]

seat　seat　seat　seat

station
역, 정거장

[stéiʃən 스때이션]

station　station

street
거리

[strit 스뜨뤼-ㅅ]

street　street　street　street

travel
여행, 여행하다

[trǽvəl 튜뢰블]

travel　travel　travel　travel

trip
여행

[trip 츄뤄ㅂ]

trip　trip　trip　trip

- Please, have a seat. 　　　　　　앉으세요.
- I wait for taxi at the station. 　　나는 정거장에서 택시를 기다린다.
- Let's cross the street. 　　　　　길을 건너자.
- I want to travel around the world. 나는 전세계를 여행하고 싶어요.
- How was your trip? 　　　　　　이거 해보자!(이거 시도해보자)

12. 언 어

and
그리고, ~와
[ænd 앤드]

and and and and and

ask
묻다, 질문하다
[æsk 애스크]

ask ask ask ask

because
왜냐하면
[bikɔ́ːz 비커-즈]

because because because

but
그러나, 하지만
[bʌt 벗]

but but but but but

- I like hamburger and pizza.

- "What are you doing?" Mom asked.

- I like Tom because he is kind.

- He likes apples. But I don't.

나는 햄버거와 피자를 좋아해.

"뭐하고 있니?" 엄마가 물어보셨어요.

나는 Tom이 좋아요. 왜냐하면 친절하니까요.

그는 사과를 좋아해요. 그러나 저는 안 좋아해요.

bye
(헤어질 때)안녕

[bai 바이]

bye bye bye bye

dictionary
사전

[dikʃəneri딕셔네뤼]

dictionary   dictionary

example
보기, 예

[igzǽmpl
이그젬쁠]

example example example

hear
듣다

[hiər 히얼]

hear hear hear hear hear

hello
안녕, 여보세요

[helóu 헬로우]

hello   hello   hello

- "Good bye~ see you later."
- Can I borrow your dictionary?
- Can you give me an example?
- Can you hear me?
- "Hello, may I speak to Tom?"

"안녕~ 다음에 보자"
당신의 사전을 빌릴 수 있을까요?
예를 하나 들어볼래?
내말 들리니?
여보세요, tom이랑 통화할 수 있을까요?

49

how
어떻게, 얼마나
[hau 하우]

how　how　how　how

idea
생각
[aidíːə 아이디어]

idea idea idea idea

listen
듣다
[lísn 리쓴]

listen　listen　listen　listen

matter
문제, 곤란
[mǽtər 매터]

matter　matter　matter

question
질문
[kwéstʃən 퀘스쳔]

question　question

- How are you?   어떻게 지내니?
- Do you have any ideas?   무슨 좋은 생각 있어?
- I listen to the music everyday.   나는 매일 음악을 듣는다.
- What is the matter with you?   무슨 일이야?
- Please answer my question.   질문에 대답해 주세요.

quiz
질문, 퀴즈

[kwíz 퀴즈]

quiz   quiz   quiz

read
읽다, 낭독하다

[riːd 뤼–드]

read read read read

say
말하다

[sei 세이]

say   say   say   say   say

speak
말하다

[spiːk 스삑–ㅋ]

speak   speak   speak

spell
철자

[spel 스뺄]

spell   spell   spell   spell

- I'll give you a quiz.
- I read a book loudly.
- Don't say no.
- I can speak English.
- How do you spell this word?

내가 퀴즈 하나 낼께요.
나는 책을 큰소리로 읽었다.
안 된다고 말하지 마세요.
나는 영어를 말할 수 있어요.
이 단어의 철자가 어떻게 되나요?

story
이야기

[stɔ́ːri 스토뤼]

story   story   story   story

talk
말하다

[tɔːk 터-억]

talk talk talk talk

tell
말하다

[tel 텔]

tell   tell   tell   tell   tell

think
~라고 생각하다

[θiŋk 씽크]

think   think   think   think

what
무엇, 어떤

[hwat 왓]

what   what   what

- Mom likes to tell me some stories.
- What are you talking about?
- Don't tell a lie.
- I think it is wrong.
- What are you doing?

엄마는 나에게 얘기해 주시는 걸 좋아하신다.
너네 무슨 얘기하는 중이야?
거짓말을 하지 마라.
나는 그것이 틀렸다고 생각한다.
뭐하고 있니?

when
언제
[*h*wen 웬]

when when when when

where
어디에
[*h*wɛər 웨얼]

where where where

which
어느쪽, 어느
[*h*witʃ 윗취]

which which which which

who
누구
[*h*uː 후-]

who who who who

whom
누구를
[*h*uːm 후우-ㅁ]

whom   whom   whom

- When is your birthday?   생일이 언제야?
- Where are you from?   어디 출신이야?
- Which one is better?   어떤게 더 좋아?
- Who is he?   그는 누구야?
- Whom did you meet yesterday?   어제 누구를 만났어?

whose
누구의

[*hu*:z 후-즈]

whose whose whose

why
왜

[*h*wai 와이]

why why why why why

word
낱말, 단어

[wə:rd 워드]

word word word word

did
했다, 했었다

[did 디드]

did did did did did

- Whose daughter is she?   누구의 딸이야?
- Why do you cry?   왜 우니?
- How do you spell this word?   이 단어 철자가 어떻게 되죠?
- I did a lot of things yesterday.   어제 많은 일들을 했어요.

13. 경 제

coin
동전

[kɔin 코인]

coin coin coin coin coin

dollar
달러

[dálər 달러ㄹ]

dollar dollar dollar dollar

market
시장

[máːrkit
마ー르킷]

market market

money
돈

[mʌ́ni 머니]

money money money

- Put the coins into that machine. 저 기계에 동전을 집어넣으세요.
- It's ten dollars. 10달러입니다.
- I will buy apples at market. 시장에서 사과를 살 거예요.
- How much money do you have? 넌 돈이 얼마 있니?

pay
지불하다
[pei 페이]

pay pay pay pay pay

shop
가게
[ʃap 샵]

shop shop shop shop

store
가게, 상점
[stɔːr 스또어-ㄹ]

store store store

supermarket
슈퍼마켓
[súːpərmáːrkit 수-퍼ㄹ말킷]

supermatket supermatket

- We pay the school expenses.
- I went to the toy shop.
- I came by a fruit store.
- I went to a supermarket to buy corn.

우리는 학비를 낸다.

나는 장난감가게로 갔다.

나는 과일 가게에 들렀다.

나는 옥수수를 사기 위해 슈퍼마켓에 갔다.

14. 동 물

animal
동물, 짐승
[ǽnəməl
애니멀]

animal   animal   animal

ant
개미
[ænt 앤트]

ant   ant   ant   ant

bird
새
[bəːrd 버얼드]

bird   bird   bird   bird

chicken
닭
[tʃíkən 취킨]

chicken   chicken   chicken

- A bear is a big animal.
- The ants are diligent.
- Birds fly in the air.
- The chickens make a lot of noise.

곰은 몸집이 큰 동물이에요.

개미들은 부지런하다.

새들은 공중을 날아다녀요.

닭들이 너무나 시끄럽게 해요.

cow
암소, 젖소

[kau 카우]

cow cow cow cow cow

deer
사슴

[diər 디얼]

deer deer deer

duck
오리

[dʌk 덕]

duck duck duck duck

elephant
코끼리

[éləfənt 엘러풔ㄴ트]

elephant elephant

fish
물고기

[fiʃ 퓌쉬]

fish fish fish fish

- Cows make milk."   암소들은 우유를 만들어요.
- Have you ever seen a deer?   사슴을 본 적이 있니?
- The ducks can't fly.   오리는 날 수 없다.
- The elephants are very strong.   코끼리는 매우 힘이 세다.
- Did you catch any fish?   고기 좀 잡으셨어요?

fly (2)
파리
[flai 플롸이]

fly　fly　fly　fly　fly　fly

fox
여우
[fɑks 팍스]

fox　fox　fox　fox　fox　fox

hen
암탉
[hen 헨]

hen　hen　hen　hen

horse
말
[hɔːrs 호올스]

horse　horse　horse

monkey
원숭이
[mʌ́ŋki 멍끼]

monkey　monkey

- Frog eats fly.
- A fox is a wild animal.
- Hen lays an egg.
- Riding a horse is very funny.
- Monkeys like bananas.

개구리는 파리를 먹어요.
여우는 야생 동물이다.
암탉은 계란을 낳아요.
말타는 건 재밌어요.
원숭이들은 바나나를 좋아해요.

pig
돼지

[pig 픽]

pig pig pig pig pig

sheep
양

[ʃiːp 쉽]

sheep sheep sheep sheep

tiger
호랑이

[táigər 타이걸]

tiger tiger tiger

zoo
동물원

[zuː 주-]

zoo zoo zoo zoo zoo zoo

- Pigs eat a lot.
- I have never seen sheep.
- Have you ever seen a tiger?
- Let's go to the zoo.

돼지는 많이 먹어요.
나는 양을 본 적이 없어요.
너는 호랑이를 본 적 있니?
동물원에 가자.

15. 때 · 계절 · 방향

afternoon
오후
[ǽftərnúːn
애프터ㄹ누-운]

afternoon   afternoon

autumn
가을
[ɔ́ːtəm 어-틈]

autumn   autumn

date
날짜
[deit 데잇트]

date   date   date

day
낮, 하루
[dei 데이]

day day day day day day

- I met him in the afternoon.   나는 그를 오후에 만났어요.
- It is windy in the autumn.   가을에는 바람이 많이 불어요.
- What's the date today?   오늘 몇일이에요?(오늘 날짜가 어떻게 되죠?)
- I play all day long every day.   난 매일 하루 종일 놀아요.

east
동쪽

[iːst 이스트]

east   east   east

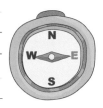

evening
저녁

[íːvniŋ 이-브닝]

evening   evening

fall
가을

[fɔːl 풔ㄹ]

fall fall fall fall fall fall

holiday
휴일, 공휴일

[hálədéi
할러데이]

holiday   holiday   holiday

hour
시간

[auəɾ 아우월]

hour   hour   hour

- Go east.
- I feel tired in the evening.
- In fall, we can see many leaves.
- Did you have a good holiday?
- Peter slept for five hours.

동쪽으로 가.
나는 저녁에는 피곤해.
가을에는 낙엽을 많이 볼 수 있어요.
휴일 잘 보내셨어요?
Peter는 5시간동안 잤어요.

lunch
점심
[lɔntʃ 런취]

lunch lunch lunch lunch

map
지도
[mæp 맵]

map　map　map　map

minute
분
[mínit 미닛]

minute　minute　minute

morning
아침
[mɔ́ːrniŋ 모-ㄹ닝]

morning　morning

night
밤
[nait 나잇]

night　night　night

- It's time for lunch.　점심 먹을 시간이에요.
- I marked my house on the map.　우리(나의)집을 지도에 표시했다.
- We have only 5 minutes.　우리는 오직 5분의 시간이 없어(우리는 5분밖에 시간이 없어).
- Good morning!　좋은 아침!
- I stayed up all night.　나는 밤새도록 깨어 있었다.

noon
정오, 한 낮

[nuːn 눈]

noon   noon   noon   noon

north
북쪽

[nɔːrθ 노-ㄹ쓰]

north   north   north   north

season
계절

[síːzn 씨-즌]

season   season   season

south
남쪽

[sauθ 싸웃쓰]

south   south   south

spring
봄

[spriŋ 스프링]

spring spring spring

- We have lunch at noon.
- My house stands in the north of Seoul.
- What's your favorite season?
- The man went south.
- I like spring.

우리는 정오에 점심을 먹는다.
우리 집은 서울의 북쪽에 있다.
가장 좋아하는 계절은?
그는 남쪽으로 갔다.
난 봄이 좋아요.

64

summer
여름
[sʌ́mər 써머ㄹ]

summer   summer

today
오늘
[tudéi 투데이]

today today today today

tomorrow
내일
[təmɔ́ːrou 투머-로우]

tomorrow   tomorrow

tonight
오늘 밤
[tənáit 터나잇]

tonight   tonight   tonight

visit
방문하다
[vízit 뷔짓]

visit   visit   visit   visit

- In summer, it is hot.
- Today is my birthday.
- Tomorrow will be cold.
- Tonight will be snowy.
- Can you visit me, today?

여름에는 더워요.
여름에는 더워요.
내일은 추울 거야.
오늘밤엔 눈이 올 거야.
오늘 절 방문해 줄 수 있나요?

way
길, 방법

[wei 웨이]

way way way way

week
주, 1주간

[wi:k 위-크]

week week week week

west
서쪽

[west 웨스트]

west west west west

winter
겨울

[wíntər 윈터얼]

winter winter winter

yesterday
어제

[jéstərdéi 예스털데이]

yesterday yesterday

- There is no way through.   통로가 없어요.
- I will travel America for a week.   나는 일주일동안 미국을 여행할 거야.
- The sun sets in the west.   해는 서쪽으로 진다.
- It's cold in winter.   겨울엔 추워요.
- Yesterday was my brother's birthday.   어제는 내 남동생의 생일이었다.

16. 우주 · 자연

air
공기

[ɛər 에어ㄹ]

air　air　air　air　air

beach
물가, 바닷가

[biːtʃ 비-잇취]

beach　beach　beach　beach

cloud
구름

[klaud클라우드]

cloud　cloud　cloud

country
나라, 지역

[kʌ́ntri컨츠뤼]

country　country　country

- We would die without air.　　우리는 공기가 없으면 죽고 말 거야.
- We will go to beach.　　나는 올 여름 바닷가에 가고 싶어요.
- The birds fly over the clouds.　　새들이 구름 위로 날아다녀요.
- My grandmother lives in the country.　　할머니는 시골에서 사셔요.

earth
지구, 땅

[əːrθ 어-ㄹ쓰]

earth earth earth earth

field
들판

[fiːld 퓌-ㄹ드]

field field field field

grass
풀

[græs 그뢰쓰]

grass grass grass grass

gold
금

[gould 고울드]

gold gold gold gold

green
녹색

[griːn 그뤼인]

green green green green

- There are a lot of animals on the earth.
- The farmer works in the field.
- "Keep off the grass."
- This box is full of gold.
- I like green color.

지구에는 많은 동물들이 있어요.
농부가 들판에서 일을 해요.
잔디에 들어가지 마시오.
이 상자는 금으로 가득 차 있어요.
저는 녹색을 좋아해요.

ground
땅, 운동장

[graund 그롸운드]

ground   ground

hill
언덕

[hil 힐]

hill hill hill hill hill hill

island
섬

[áilənd아일런드]

island island island

jungle
밀림, 정글

[dʒʌ́ŋgl 쥐ㅇ글]

jungle jungle jungle jungle

light(2)
빛, 조명

[lait 라잇트]

light   light   light   light

- Let's play at the ground.
- A cottage is on a hill.
- I have never been to the island.
- The lion is king of the jungle.
- Don't forget to turn off the light.

운동장에서 놀자.
언덕 위에 작은집이 하나 있다.
나는 그 섬에 가본 적이 없어요.
사자는 밀림의 왕이에요.
불(조명) 끄는 것 잊지 마!

lake
호수

[leik 레익]

lake lake lake lake

land
땅, 육지

[lænd 랜드]

land land land land

leaf
나뭇잎

[liːf 리-프]

leaf leaf leaf leaf leaf leaf

mountain
산

[mauntən 마운튼]

mountain mountain

plant
식물

[plænt 플랜트]

plant plant plant plant

- There are many lakes in Canada.
- I traveld over land and sea last year.
- Look! The red leaf is falling.
- I climbed a mountain last Saturday.
- The plants need water.

캐나다에는 호수가 많아요.

나는 작년에 육지와 바다를 여행했다.

봐봐! 빨간 나뭇잎이 떨어지고 있어.

나는 지난 토요일 산에 올랐어요.

식물은 물이 필요하다.

pool
웅덩이, 연못

[puːl 푸-울]

pool pool pool pool pool

rain
비, 비가오다

[rein 뤠인]

rain rain rain rain

rainbow
무지개

[réinbóu 뤠인보우]

rainbow rainbow rainbow

river
강

[rívər뤼버-ㄹ]

river river river

sand
모래

[sænd 쌘드]

sand sand sand sand

- Fish are in the pool.
- I walked in the rain.
- we can see a rainbow after it rains.
- I jumped into the river.
- We built sand castles.

연못에 물고기들이 있어요.

나는 빗속을 걸었어요.

비가 오고 난 후에는 무지개를 볼 수 있다.

나는 강에 뛰어 들었어요.

우리는 모래성을 쌓았다.

sea
바다

[siː 씨-]

sea   sea   sea   sea

silver
은, 은빛, 은의

[sílvər 씰뷔얼]

silver   silver   silver   silver

snow
눈, 눈이오다

[snou 스노우]

snow   snow   snow

space
공간, 우주

[speis 스뻬이스]

space   space   space   space

star
별

[staːr 스따-ㄹ]

star   star   star   star

- I went to the sea last summer.
- He gave me a silver ring.
- It is snowing.
- The people are looking for a parking space.
- It is hard to see stars in the city.

나는 지난 여름에 바다에 갔어요.
그는 나에게 은반지를 주었다.
눈이 오고 있다.
사람들이 주차할 공간을 찾고 있다.
도시에서는 별을 보기 힘들다.

sun
태양, 햇빛

[sʌn 썬]

sun sun sun sun sun

water
물

[wɔ́:tər 워-터]

water water water

wind
바람

[wind 윈드]

wind wind wind

wood
나무, 숲

[wud 우드]

wood wood wood wood

world
세계, 지구

[wə:rld 워-ㄹ드]

world world world world

- The sun rises in the east. | 해는 동쪽에서 뜬다.
- People drink water every day. | 사람들은 물을 매일 마신다.
- The paper is swing in the wind. | 그 종이가 바람에 흔들린다.
- I walked in the wood. | 나는 숲속을 걸었어요.
- I want to travel all over the world. | 나는 전 세계를 여행하고 싶다.

73

17. 움직임을 나타내는 단어

appear
나타나다

[əpíər 어피얼]

appear   appear   appear

arrive
도착하다

[əráiv어롸이브]

arrive   arrive   arrive

blow
불다

[blou 블로우]

blow blow blow blow blow

break
부수다

[breik 브뢰익크]

break   break   break   break

- He appears in the room.   그가 방에 나타났다(들어왔다).
- Dad will arrive soon.   도착하실꺼야.
- My father is blowing up balloons.   아빠가 풍선을 불고 계셔요.
- A glass is easy to break.   유리는 깨지기 쉽다.

bring
가져오다

[briŋ 브링]

bring bring bring

broke
깨트렸다

[brouk브로-크]

broke broke broke broke

build
세우다, 짓다

[bild 빌드]

build build build build

burn
타다, 태우다

[bəːrn버-ㄹ언]

burn burn burn burn

call
부르다

[kɔːl 커얼]

call call call call

- Bring me the book, please.
- I broke my grandma's glasses.
- I want to build a doghouse.
- Mom burned the steaks today.
- My friends call me Sunny.

그 책 좀 가져다 주렴.
내가 할머니의 안경을 깨뜨렸다.
나는 개집을 짓고 싶어요.
엄마는 오늘 스테이크를 태웠어요.
친구들은 저를 Sunny라고 불러요.

75

carry
운반하다
[kǽri 캐뤼]

carry carry carry carry

catch
잡다, 받다
[kætʃ 캣춰]

catch catch catch catch

close
닫다
[klouz클로우즈]

close close close close

count
수를 세다
[kaunt 카운트]

count count count count

cross
가로지르다
[crɔːs 크뤄스]

cross cross cross cross

- I always carry schoolbag.
- Cats are very good at catching mice.
- Close one eye and look at that.
- Let's count to 10! 1, 2, 3...
- Let's cross the street.

저는 항상 책가방을 가지고 다녀요.
고양이는 쥐를 아주 잘 잡아요.
한쪽 눈을 감고 저것을 봐봐.
10까지 세어보자! 일, 이, 삼...
길을 건너자.

cry
소리치다, 울다

[krai 크롸이]

cry   cry   cry   cry

cut
베다, 깎다

[kʌt 컷]

cut   cut   cut   cut   cut

die
죽다

[dai 다이]

die die die die die die

drink
마시다

[driŋk 쥬링크]

drink drink drink

drive
운전하다

[draiv 드롸이브]

drive drive drive

- "Why are you crying?"
- I had cut my finger.
- That sick dog will die.
- If you are thirsty, drink some water.
- Can you drive a car?

왜 울고 있니?
나는 손가락을 베었다.
저 아픈 개는 죽을거야.
목이 마르면 물을 좀 마시세요.
차 운전할 줄 알아요?

drop
떨어뜨리다

[drap 드롸ㅂ]

drop　drop　drop　drop

eat
먹다

[iːt 이-잇]

eat　eat　eat　eat

enjoy
즐기다

[éndʒɔ́i 엔줘이]

enjoy　enjoy　enjoy

excite
흥분시키다

[iksáit 익싸이트]

excite excite excite excite

excuse
용서하다

[ikskjúːz 익스큐즈]

excuse　excuse　excuse

- "Don't drop the dishes."
- I like to eat salads.
- My dad enjoys driving.
- The game excited us.
- Excuse me.

접시 떨어뜨리지 마라.
샐러드 먹는 걸 좋아해요.
아빠는 운전을 즐기셔요.
그 시합은 우리를 흥분시켰다.
실례합니다

feel
느끼다

[fiːl 퓌-일]

feel　feel　feel　feel　feel

fight
싸우다

[fait 퐈잇트]

fight　fight　fight　fight

fill
채우다

[fil 퓔]

fill　fill　fill　fill　fill

find
찾다, 발견하다

[faind 퐈인드]

find　find　find　find　find

finish
끝내다, 마치다

[fíniʃ 퓌니쉬]

finish　finish　finish　finish

- I feel the summer is coming.
- Sometimes I fight with my brother.
- Fill in the blank.
- I can't find my doll.
- Let's finish it today.

여름이 오고있는 게 느껴져요.
가끔 동생이랑 싸워요.
빈칸을 채우세요.
제 인형을 찾을 수가 없어요..
오늘 그걸 끝냅시다.

fix
수리하다

[fiks 퓌ㄱ스]

fix   fix   fix   fix   fix   fix

fly(1)
날다

[flai 플롸이]

fly   fly   fly   fly   fly

forget
잊다

[fərgét 폴겟]

forget forget forget forget

happen
발생하다

[hǽpən 해쁜]

happen   happen   happen

have
가지고 있다

[hæv 해브]

have   have   have

- Dad and I will fix the roof today.
- I can't fly.
- Did you forget to buy some apples?
- How did it happen?
- I have a lot of stamps.

아빠랑 오늘 지붕을 고칠꺼에요.
나는 날 수 없어요.
사과 사는 거 잊으셨어요?
어떻게 그 일이 발생했나요?
저는 우표를 아주 많이 가지고 있어요.

help
돕다
[help 헬-프]

help help help help

hit
때리다
[hit 힛]

hit hit hit hit hit hit

hide
숨기다, 숨다
[haid 하이드]

hide hide hide hide

hold
잡다, 붙들다
[hould 호울드]

hold hold hold hold hold

hope
바라다
[houp 호웁]

hope hope hope hope

- Help me, please!
- Don't hit me!
- Don't hide my doll.
- "Hold my hand!", he cries.
- I hope you have a good time.

저를 도와주세요!
나를 때리지 마.
내 인형 숨기지마!!
"내 손을 잡아!" 그가 외쳤어요.
좋은 시간되시길 바랍니다.

hurry
서두르다
[hə:ri 허-뤼]

hurry hurry hurry hurry

hurt
다치게 하다
[hə:rt 허-ㄹ트]

hurt hurt hurt hurt hurt

keep
계속하다
[ki:p 키-입]

keep keep keep keep

kick
차다
[kik 킥]

kick kick kick kick

kill
죽이다, 없애다
[kil 킬]

kill kill kill kill kill kill

- Hurry up, or we'll be late.
- I am badly hurt.
- Keep your room clean.
- Tom kicked a ball.
- Cats kill the mouse.

서둘러! 안 그러면 늦을꺼야.
난 심하게 다쳤어요.
당신의 방을 깨끗히 유지하세요.
Tom은 공을 찼어요.
고양이는 쥐를 죽여요.

knock
두드리다

[nak 낙]

knock　knock　knock

know
알다, 이해하다

[nou 노우]

know　know　know　know

jump
뛰어오르다

[dʒʌmp 줘ㅁ프]

jump　jump　jump

laugh
웃다

[læf 래프]

laugh　laugh　laugh　laugh

let
시키다

[let 렛]

let　let　let　let　let　let

- I knocked the door.
- Do you know what I mean?
- Teddy is ready to jump up.
- He laughs loudly.
- I let him go out.

전 노크를 했어요.

내가 무슨 말 하는 지 알겠어?

Teddy는 뛰어오를 준비가 되었어요

그는 큰 소리로 웃었어요.

그를 나가게 했어요.

like
좋아하다
[laik 라이크]

like   like   like   like   like

look
보다
[luk 룩]

look   look   look

love
사랑하다
[lɔv 러브]

love   love   love   love   love

make
만들다
[meik 메이크]

make   make   make   make

may
~해도 좋다
[mei 메이]

may   may   may   may

- I like dancing.
- Look at it. Do you know what it is?
- Mom and dad love each other.
- I made a cake for my mother.
- You may go now.

저는 춤추는 걸 좋아해요.
이것 좀 봐. 이게 뭔지 알어?
엄마 아빠는 서로를 사랑하셔요.
나는 어머니를 위해 케이크를 만들었어요.
넌 이제 가도 좋다.

meet
만나다
[miːt 미잇트]

meet   meet   meet

move
움직이다
[muːv 무-브]

move   move   move   move

must
꼭 해야만 한다
[mʌst 머스트]

must   must   must   must

pass
지나가다
[pæs 패스]

pass   pass   pass   pass

pick
따다
[pik 픽]

pick   pick   pick   pick   pick

- I am glad to meet you.
- We moved to a new house.
- You must do this.
- I passed through the park.
- Please, pick one of them.

· 만나게 되어서 기뻐요.
  우리는 새집으로 이사했어요.
  당신은 이것을 해야만 한다.
  나는 공원을 가로질러 지나갔다.
  그것들 중 하나를 고르세요.

play
연주하다, 놀다

[plei 플레이]

play play play play

please
기쁘게 하다

[pliːz 플리이즈]

please please please

put
놓다, 두다

[put 풋]

put put put put put

record
기록하다

[rikɔ́ːrd 뢰커-ㄹ드]

record record record

remember
기억하다

[rimémbər 뤼멤버얼]

remember remember

- She plays the violin very well.   그녀는 바이올린 연주를 매우 잘한다.
- I am pleased to see you.   너를 보게 되어 기뻐.
- I put some flowers into the vase.   꽃병에 꽃 몇 송이를 넣었다.
- I record everything in this note.   나는 모든 것을 이 노트에 기록한다.
- I remember her.   나는 그녀를 기억한다.

ride
타다
[raid 롸이드]

ride ride ride ride ride

ring
울리다
[riŋ 링]

ring ring ring ring ring

run
달리다
[rʌn 뤄ㄴ]

run run run run run

see
보다
[siː 씨–]

see see see see

send
보내다
[send 쎈드]

send send send send

- Can you ride a bicycle?
- The telephone is ringing.
- I like to run.
- I want to see you!
- I will send you an e-mail.

자전거 탈 줄 아니?
전화가 울리고 있어요.
나는 달리는 걸 좋아해요.
네가 보고싶어!
나는 너에게 e-mail을 보낼 것이다.

shall
~일 것이다

[ʃæl 쉘]

shall   shall   shall   shall

shoot
쏘다, 던지다

[ʃuːt 슛]

shoot   shoot   shoot   shoot

shout
소리치다

[ʃaut 샤웃]

shout   shout   shout   shout

show
보이다

[ʃou 쇼우]

show   show   show   show

slide
미끄러지다

[slaid슬라이드]

slide slide slide slide slide

- I shall be very happy to see you.
- He tried to shoot a bird.
- Don't shout to your brother.
- Can you show it to me?
- She slid on the ice.

너를 보게 되면 매우 기쁠 거야.
그는 새 한 마리를 쏘려고 하였다.
동생에게 소리치지 마라.
그것을 내게 보여줄 수 있니?
그녀는 얼음판 위에서 미끄러졌다.

smell
냄새맡다
[smel 스멜]

smell　smell　smell　smell

smile
웃다, 미소지다
[smail 스마일]

smile　smile　smile

spend
낭비하다
[spend 스뺀드]

spend spend spend spend

strike
때리다
[straik스뜨롸익]

strike　strike　strike　strike

taste
맛을 보다
[teist테이스트]

taste　taste　taste　taste

- It smells good.   좋은 냄새가 난다.
- She smiled at me.   그녀가 나를 보고 웃었다.
- How much money do you spend?   돈을 얼마나 썼니?
- I strike a ball.   나는 공을 친다.
- It tastes sweet.   단맛이 난다.

throw
던지다
[θrou 쓰로우]

throw throw throw throw

wait
기다리다
[weit 웨잇]

wait wait wait wait wait

walk
걷다, 산책하다
[wɔːk 워-억]

walk walk walk

- The pitcher threw a ball to me.   투수가 나에게 공을 던졌어요.

- Min-ho is waiting for his girl friend.   민호는 그의 여자 친구를 기다립니다.

- I walk in the park with my wife everyday.   나는 매일 아내와 공원을 걷는다.

18. 모 양

angry
화난
[ǽŋgri 앵그뤼]

angry　angry　angry

any
무엇이든
[éni 애니]

any　any　any　any　any

beautiful
아름다운
[bjúːtəfəl 뷰-러플]

beautiful　　beautiful

busy
바쁜
[bízi 비지]

busy　busy　busy

- Tom looks angry.
- Do you have any questions?
- Snow white is beautiful.
- My parents are busy.

Tom이 화난 것 같아.

무슨 질문이 있나요?

백설공주는 예뻐요.

우리 부모님은 바쁘셔요.

careful
조심스러운

[kέərfəl 캐어ㄹ풀]

careful careful careful

close
가까운, 친한

[klous 클로우즈]

close close close close

enough
충분한

[inʌ́f 이너프]

enough enough enough

every
모든

[évriː 에브뤼]

every every every

few
거의 없는

[fjuː 퓨-]

few few few few few few

- Be careful not to drop the cup.
- Tom and Jerry are very close friends.
- I think that's enough.
- Everyone likes him.
- I have few cards.

컵을 떨어뜨리지 않게 조심해.
Tom과 Jerry는 아주 친한 친구 사이예요.
그거면 충분하다고 생각해.
모두 그를 좋아해요.
나는 카드도 별로 없어요.

foolish
어리석은
[fúːliʃ 푸-울리쉬]

foolish foolish foolish

free
자유로운
[friː 프뤼-]

free free free free free

fresh
새로운, 신선한
[freʃ 프뤳쉬]

fresh fresh fresh fresh

full
가득한, 충만한
[ful 풀]

full full full full

good
좋은, 착한
[gud 굿]

good good good good

- It was a foolish idea.
- What do you do in your free time?
- These vegetables look fresh.
- The box is full of books.
- I think it is a good idea.

그건 어리석은 생각이었어요.
한가할 때 뭐하세요?
이 야채들은 신선해 보여요.
이 박스에는 책이 가득 들어있다.
좋은 생각인 것 같아요.

hard
딱딱한, 어려운

[ha:rd 하알드]

hard   hard   hard   hard

hungry
배고픈

[hʌ́ŋgri 헝그뤼]

hungry   hungry

kind
친절한

[kaind 카인드]

kind   kind   kind   kind   kind

late
늦은, 늦게

[leit 레잇]

late   late   late   late   late

lonely
외로운

[lóunlí 로운리]

lonely lonely lonely lonely

- It is very hard to solve this problem.
- I'm very hungry.
- The police officer is very kind.
- Let's meet at 7 o'clock. Don't be late.
- I feel lonely.

이 문제를 해결하는 건 어려워요.
나 정말 배고파요.
그 경찰관은 매우 친절해요.
7시에 만나자. 늦지마!
나는 외롭다.

94

new
새로운

[nju: 뉴-]

new new new new

next
다음의, 다음에

[nekst 넥스트]

next next next next next

nice
멋진

[nais 나이스]

nice nice nice nice

only
오직, 유일한

[óunli 오운리]

only only only only only

poor
가난한, 불쌍한

[puər 푸얼]

poor poor poor

- I wear a new uniform.
- See you next time.
- This jacket is very nice.
- She is an only daughter.
- He is a poor man.

나는 새로운 교복을 입는다.
다음에 보자.
이 자켓은 매우 멋져요.
그녀는 외동딸이야.
그는 불쌍한 사람이다.

quiet
조용한
[kwáiət 콰이엇-트]

quiet   quiet   quiet

ready
준비가 된
[rédi 뢰디]

ready   ready   ready

round
둥근, 동그란
[raund 롸운드]

round round round round

sad
슬픈, 슬퍼하는
[sæd 쌔드]

sad   sad   sad   sad

safe
안전한
[seif 쎄이프]

safe safe safe safe safe

- Be quiet!
- Are you ready to order?
- There is a round table.
- I am very sad.
- There is a safe place.

조용히 해!
주문할 준비 되셨어요?
거기 둥근 탁자가 있다.
그는 불쌍한 사람이다.
안전한 장소다.

same
동일한, 똑같은

[seim 쎄임]

same   same   same   same

sorry
죄송한

[sɔ́ːri 써-뤼]

sorry   sorry   sorry   sorry

stupid
어리석은

[stjúːpid 스뚜피-드]

stupid stupid stupid stupid

thank
감사하다

[θæŋk 쌩크]

thank   thank   thank

wet
젖은, 축축한

[wet 웨트]

wet   wet   wet   wet

- We have the same caps.
- I am sorry to hear that.
- He is stupid.
- Thank you very much.
- We have the wet season in June.

우리는 똑같은 모자를 가지고 있다.
그것 참 유감이에요.
그는 어리석다.
정말 감사합니다.
6월은 장마철이다.

19. 대립어 (단어의 대립 관계는 의미의 대립 관계보다 사전적 대립 관계임

thin
얇은

[θin 띤]

thin thin thin thin

thick
두꺼운

[θik 씩]

thick   thick   thick

heavy
무거운

[hévi 헤뷔]

heavy heavy heavy

light(1)
가벼운

[lait 라잇트]

light   light   light

- This book is very thin.
- How thick is it?
- Elephants are really heavy.
- Tom is lighter than his brother.

이 책은 정말 얇아요.

그건 두께가 얼마나 되죠?

코끼리는 아주 무겁다.

Tom은 그의 형보다 가벼워요.

quick
빠른

[kw ik 퀵]

quick   quick   quick   quick

slow
느린

[slou 슬로우]

slow   slow   slow

far
멀리

[faːr 파-ㄹ]

far   far   far   far   far

near
가까운

[niər 니얼]

near   near   near   near

poor
가난한

[púər 푸얼]

poor poor poor poor

- He is quick to learn.   그는 배우는 속도가 빠르다.
- The turtle is slow.   거북이는 느리다.
- My house is far from here.   우리집은 여기서 멀어요.
- Our house stands near my school.   우리집은 학교 옆에 있어요.
- She always helps the poor.   그녀는 항상 가난한 이들을 돕는다.

rich
돈 많은

[ritʃ 륏취]

rich   rich   rich   rich

start
출발하다

[staːrt 스딸-ㅌ]

start   start   start   start

stop
멈추다

[stap 스땁]

stop   stop   stop   stop

dirty
더러운, 불결한

[dɔ́ːrti 더-ㄹ티]

dirty dirty dirty dirty dirty

clean
깨끗한

[kliːn 클리인]

clean   clean   clean   clean

- He is very rich.
- Let's start.
- He stopped to talk.
- My brother's room is dirty all the time.
- I clean my room everyday.

그는 매우 부유하다.
시작하자.
그는 이야기하기 위해 멈췄다.
내 동생 방은 항상 더러워요.
저는 제방을 매일 청소해요.

100

in
~안에

[in 인]

in in in in in in

out
밖으로, 밖에

[aut 아웃]

out out out out out

push
밀다

[puʃ 푸쉬]

push push push push

pull
당기다

[pul 풀]

pull pull pull pull

sit
앉다

[sit 씻]

sit sit sit sit sit sit

- There is a cat in the box.
- Let's go out.
- Push the door open.
- Pull the door open.
- Sit down, please.

상자 안에 고양이 한 마리가 있다.
우리 밖으로 나가자.
문을 밀어서 열어요.
문을 당겨서 열어요.
앉아 주세요.

stand
서다, 일어서다

[stænd 스땐드]

stand stand stand stand

open
열다

[óupən 오우쁜]

open open open

shut
닫다, 덮다

[ʃʌt 셧]

shut shut shut shut shut

glad
기쁜, 반가운

[glæd 글래드]

glad glad glad glad

sad
슬 픈

[sǽd 쌔에드]

sad sad sad sad

- Stand up, please.
- Open the door, please.
- Please shut the window.
- I'm glad to meet you.
- She looks sad.

일어서 주세요.
문좀 열어 주세요.
창문 좀 닫아 주세요.
만나서 반가워.
그녀는 슬퍼보여.

find
찾다

[faind 파인드]

find　find　find　find　find

lose
잃다

[luːz 루-즈]

lose　lose　lose　lose　lose

ugly
못생긴, 추한

[ʌ́gli 어글리]

ugly　ugly　ugly　ugly

beautiful
아름다운

[bjúːtəfəl 뷰-티플]

beautiful　　beautiful

full
가득 찬

[ful 풀]

full　full　full　full　full

- You can find strawberries in the wood.
- Don't lose the money.
- This dog has an ugly face.
- This poem is really beautiful.
- Do not talk with your mouth full.

숲에서 딸기를 찾을 수 있을 거예요.
돈 잃어버리지 마라.
이 강아지는 참 못생겼어요.
이 시는 정말 아름답군요.
입에 음식을 가득 물고 말하지 마라.

empty
빈
[émpti 엠띠]

empty   empty   empty

late
늦은
[leit 레잇]

late   late   late   late

early
이른, 일찍
[ə́ːrli 어–ㄹ리]

early   early   early   early

arrive
도착하다, 닿다
[əráiv 어롸이브]

arrive   arrive   arrive

depart
떠나다
[dipaːrt 디파트]

depart   depart   depart

- Why is my basket empty?
- Why are you so late?
- I got up early this morning.
- The letter arrived this morning.
- The plane to Busan will depart at 1:00.

왜 내 바구니가 텅 비었지?
너 왜 그렇게 늦니?
오늘 아침엔 일찍 일어났어요.
편지가 오늘 아침에 왔어요.
부산행 비행기는 1시에 떠난다.

same 같은 [seim 쎄임]	same same same same
different 다른 [difərənt 디퍼런트]	different different
love 사랑하다 [lʌv 러브]	love love love love
hate 싫어하다 [heit 헤잇트]	hate hate hate hate
small 작은 [smɔːl 스모-ㄹ]	small small small small

- Tom's and I are the same age.
- I need a different pen.
- I love you, Mom.
- I hate mouse.
- The ball is small.

톰과 나는 동갑이에요.
나 다른 펜이 필요해.
엄마, 사랑해요.
난 쥐를 싫어해.
그 공은 작다.

big
큰, 커다란
[big 빅]

big big big big big

go
가다
[gou 고우]

go go go go go

come
오다
[kʌm 컴]

come come come come

forward
앞으로
[fɔ́rwərd 풔어드]

forward forward forward

back
뒤로, 거꾸로
[bæk 백]

back back back back

- An elephant is a big animal.   코끼리는 몸집이 큰 동물이예요.
- I go to school everyday.   나는 매일 학교에 간다.
- Grandfather will come next Friday.   할아버지는 다음 주 금요일 날 오실거예요.
- He took two steps forward.   그가 앞으로 두 걸음을 뗐다.
- Is there something on my back?   제 등에 뭐가 있나요?

finish
끝내다

[fíniʃ 퓌니쉬]

finish　finish　finish　finish

start
시작하다

[staːrt스딸-트]

start　start　start　start

hard
단단한, 딱딱한

[haːrd 하알드]

hard　hard　hard　hard

soft
부드러운

[soːft 써-트]

soft　soft　soft　soft

last
마지막의, 지난

[læst 레스트]

last　last　last　last

- Have you finished your dinner?
- Let's start.
- This bread is very hard.
- A baby has soft skin.
- It is your last chance!

저녁은 다 드셨나요?
시작하자.
이 빵은 정말 딱딱하네요.
아기는 피부가 보들보들해요.
이번이 너에게 마지막 기회야.

first
처음의
[fə:rst 풔스트]

first   first   first   first

fast
빠른
[fæst 풰스트]

fast   fast   fast   fast

slow
느린
[slóu 슬로우]

slow slow slow slow slow

buy
사다, 구입하다
[bai 바이]

buy buy buy buy buy buy

sell
팔다
[sel 쎌]

sell sell sell sell sell sell

- He was the first arrival.
- It is very fast train.
- Will you slow down?
- I buy some chocolate at the store.
- He sells cars.

그가 처음으로 도착했다.
이건 굉장히 빠른 기차예요.
좀 천천히 할래?
나는 가게에서 초콜릿을 삽니다.
그는 자동차를 판다.

bad
나쁜

[bǽd 베드]

bad   bad   bad   bad

good
좋은, 착한

[gud 굿]

good   good   good   good

give
주다

[gív 기브]

give   give   give   give

take
받다

[teik 테익]

take   take   take   take   take

expensive
비싼

[ikspénsiv 익스펜시브]

expensive   expensive

- I feel bad today.
- Read a good book.
- Please, give me that book.
- Take this letter to your mother.
- Isn't this pretty expensive.

난 오늘 기분이 나빠.
좋은 책을 읽으세요.
그 책을 좀 줘.
이 편지를 어머니께 가져다 드리렴.
이거 꽤 비싸지 않아?

cheap
값이 싼, 싸게

[tʃiːp 취-입]

cheap cheap cheap cheap

poor
가난한

[púər 푸얼]

poor poor poor poor

rich
돈 많은

[ritʃ 륏취]

rich rich rich rich

bright
밝은, 빛나는

[brait 브롸잇]

bright bright bright

dark
어둠, 어두운

[daːrk 다아-ㄹ크]

dark dark dark dark

- The candy was very cheap.
- She always helps the poor.
- He is very rich.
- Look on the bright side of things.
- My new skirt is dark blue.

그 사탕은 값이 쌌어요.
그녀는 항상 가난한 이들을 돕는다.
그는 매우 부유하다.
밝은 면을 봐(긍정적으로 생각하렴).
저의 새 치마는 어두운 파란색이에요.

silent
조용한
[sáiləent 싸일런트]

silent   silent   silent   silent

loud
시끄러운
[laud 라우드]

loud   loud   loud   loud

tall
키가 큰
[tɔːl 토-ㄹ]

tall   tall   tall   tall   tall

short
짧은, 키가작은
[ʃɔːrt 쇼-르트]

short   short   short   short

inside
~의 안쪽에
[insáid 인사이드]

inside inside inside inside

- He is by nature a silent boy.   그는 본래 조용한 소년이다.
- She is speaking in a loud voice.   그녀는 큰소리로 말하고 있다.
- He is tall.   그는 키가 크다.
- She is shorter than me.   그녀는 나보다 더 작아요.
- The car is inside a garage.   차는 차고 안에 있다.

outside
밖에

[áutsáid 아웃사이드]

outside   outside

hot
더운, 뜨거운

[hat 핫]

hot hot hot hot hot hot

cold
추운

[kóuld 코울드]

cold cold cold cold

long
긴

[lɔːŋ 러-엉]

long long long long

short
짧은

[ʃɔːrt 쇼트]

short   short   short   short

- It's a lovely day outside.
- I don't like hot weather.
- It's cold in winter.
- A giraffe has a long neck.
- Those pants looks too short for you.

밖에 날씨가 너무 좋아요.
나는 더운 날씨를 별로 안 좋아해요.
겨울은 추워요.
기린은 목이 길어요.
그 바지는 너에게 너무 짧게 보인다.

strong
힘이 센, 강한

[strɔːŋ 스프뤄-엉]

strong　strong　strong

weak
약한

[wiːk 위-크]

weak　weak　weak　weak

sad
슬 픈

[sǽd 쌔에드]

sad　sad　sad　sad

happy
행복한

[hǽpi 해삐]

happy happy happy happy

left
왼쪽의

[left 레프트]

left　left　left　left　left

- The boy looks strong.
- Tom is weak.
- She looks sad.
- I'm happy to be with you.
- Near the front.. on the left.

그 소년은 강해 보인다.

Tom은 (체력이)약해요.

그녀는 슬퍼보여.

너랑 있어 행복해.

앞줄 가까이 왼쪽에 있어요.

right
오른쪽

[rait 롸잇트]

 right right right

true
진실의

[trúː 트루]

true true true true true

false
거짓의

[fɔ́ːls 폴스]

false false false false

end
끝, 마치다

[end 엔드]

end end end end

start
시작, 시작하다

[staːrt 스타트]

start start start start

- Turn right.
- It is true.
- The rumor was false.
- This is the end.
- I start work at nine.

오른쪽으로 도세요.
사실이야.
그 소문은 거짓이었어.
이것으로 끝이다.
나는 아홉시에 일을 시작한다.

114

waste 낭비하다 [weist 웨이스트]	waste waste waste waste
save 절약하다 [seiv 세이브]	save save save save
dull 어리석은, 무딘 [dʌl 덜]	dull dull dull dull dull
smart 영리한 [smaːrt 스마트]	smart smart smart smart

- It is a waste of time. 그것은 시간 낭비이다.
- You must save money. 너는 돈을 절약해야만 한다.
- He has a dull sense of humor. 그는 유모 감각이 둔하다.
- She is really smart. 그녀는 정말로 영리하다.

20. 부 사

again
다시, 또
[əgén 어게인]

again again again again

also
역시, 또한
[ɔ́ːlsou 오-올쏘우]

also also also also also

always
항상, 언제나
[ɔ́ːlweiz 어-얼웨이즈]

always always

around
~의 주위에
[əráund 어롸운드]

around around around

- Do it also again.

- Tom is kind, also handsome.

- Mike is always late.

- I looked around the village.

다시 해 보렴.

Tom은 착하고, 또한 잘 생겼다.

Mike는 항상 늦는다.

저는 마을 주위를 둘러보았어요.

early
이른, 일찍

[ə́ːrli 이-ㄹ리]

early early early

else
그밖에

[els 엘스]

else else else else else

just
방금, 오직

[dʒʌst 쥐스트]

just just just just just

last
마지막으로

[læst 래스트]

last last last last last

now
지금, 방금

[nau 나우]

now now now now

- I get up early in the morning.
- "Anything else?"
- I just arrived here.
- When did you see him last?
- It is over now.

나는 아침 일찍 일어나요.
그 밖의 다른 것은요?
저는 방금 여기에 도착했어요.
마지막으로 그를 본 게 언제였죠?
이제 끝났다.

soon
곧
[suːn 쑤-운]

soon   soon   soon   soon

then
그 때, 그러면
[ðen 덴]

then then then then then

very
매우, 아주
[véri 붸뤼]

very   very   very

well
만족하게, 잘
[wel 웰]

well   well   well   well

- See you soon.   곧 보자!
- Father was a little child then.   그 당시 아버지는 작은 어린아이였다.
- I like it very much.   난 그것을 매우 좋아해요.
- He speaks English very well.   그는 영어를 아주 잘한다.

21. 전치사

about
약, 거의
[əbáut 어바웃]

about about about about

above
~의 위에
[əbʌ́v 어버브]

above above above above

after
~후에
[ǽftər애프터ㄹ]

after after after

along
~따라서
[əlɔ́:ŋ 얼러엉]

along along along along

- What is the book about?
- An airplane is flying above the clouds.
- Please repeat after me.
- Amy walked along the street.

이 책은 무엇에 관한 내용이야?

비행기가 구름 위를 날고 있다.

제가 말한 후에 따라하세요(제 말을 따라하세요).

Amy는 길을 따라 걸었다..

as
~만큼
[æz 애즈]

as as as as as as as as

at
~에서
[æt 앳]

at at at at at at

below
~보다 아래에
[bilóu 빌로우]

below below below

beside
~의 곁에
[bisáid 비싸이드]

beside beside beside

by
곁에, ~로써
[bai 바이]

by by by by by by

- Tom is as tall as I am.
- I study at home.
- Cat is below the table.
- Tom is standing beside his friends.
- I go to school by bus.

Tom은 나와 키가 같다(톰은 나와 같은 정도의 키다).
나는 집에서 공부한다.
탁자 아래 고양이가 있어요.
Tom은 친구들 옆에 서 있다.
나는 버스 타고(버스로) 학교 가요.

for
~을 위해서

[fɔːr 포-ㄹ]

for for for for for for

from
~에서

[frʌm 프럼]

from from from from from

if
(만약)~라면

[if 이프]

if if if if if if if

in
~안에

[in 인]

in in in in in in in in

- This is for you.

  이것은 너를 위한 거야.

- I'm from Japan.

  저는 일본에서 왔어요.

- If I were you, I would do my best.

  (만약)내가 너라면, 난 최선을 다할텐데.

- There is a cat in the box.

  상자 안에 고양이가 있어요.

🎒 찾아보기

dark 어둠, 어두운(110)

date 날짜(61)

day 낮, 하루(61)

deer 사슴(58)

depart 떠나다(104)

desk 책상(32)

dictionary 사전(49)

did 했다, 했었다(54)

die 죽다(77)

different 다른(105)

dinner 저녁 식사(21)

dirty 더러운, 불결한(100)

dish 접시(5)

doctor 의사(37)

dollar 달러(55)

door 문(5)

dress 의복(25)

drink 마시다(77)

drive 운전하다(77)

drop 떨어뜨리다(78)

drum 북, 드럼(28)

duck 오리(58)

dull 어리석은, 무딘(115)

e

ear 귀(9)

early 이른, 일찍(104,126)

earth 지구, 땅(68)

east 동쪽(62)

eat 먹다(78)

egg 달걀(21)

elephant 코끼리(58)

else 그밖에(117)

empty 빈(104)

end 끝, 마치다(104)

enjoy 즐기다(78)

enough 충분한(92)

eraser 지우개(32)

evening 저녁(62)

every 모든(92)

example 보기, 예(49)

excite 흥분시키다(78)

excuse 용서하다(78)

exercise 운동, 연습(27)

expensive 비싼(109)

eye 눈(10)

f

face 얼굴(10)

fall 가을(62)

false 거짓의(115)

far 멀리(99)

fast 빠른(108)

feel 느끼다(79)

few 거의 없는(92)

field 들판(68)

fight 싸우다(79)

fill 채우다(79)

film 필름, 영화(28)

find 찾다, 발견하다(79,103)

finger 손가락(10)

finish 끝내다, 마치다(79,107)

first 처음의(108)

fish 물고기(58)

fix 수리하다(80)

floor 바닥, 층(45)

fly$^{(1)}$ 날다(80)

fly$^{(2)}$ 파리(59)

food 음식(21)

foolish 어리석은(93)

foot 발(10)

for ~을 위해서(121)

forget 잊다(80)

fox 여우(59)

free 자유로운(93)

fresh 새로운, 신선한(93)

friend 친구(14)

forward 앞으로(106)

from ~에서(121)

fruit 과일(21)

full 가득한, 충만한(103)

g

game 게임 · 놀이(28)

garden 정원(6)

gas 가스(6)

gate 문, 출입구(45)

girl 소녀(14)

give 주다(109)

glad 기쁜, 반가운(102)

glass 유리, 유리컵(6)

go 가다(106)

god 하느님(38)

gold 금(68)

good 좋은, 착한(93,110)

grass 풀(68)

gray 회색, 회색의(36)

green 녹색(68)

ground 땅, 운동장(69)

group 무리, 모임, 떼(39)

h

hair 머리카락, 털(10)

hamburger 햄버거(21)

hand 손(11)

happen 발생하다(80)

happy 행복한(115)

hard 딱딱한, 어려운(94,107)

hate 싫어하다(105)

have 가지고 있다(80)

he 그는, 그가(14)

head 머리(11)

hear 듣다(49)

heart 마음, 심장(11)

heavy 무거운(98)

hello 안녕, 여보세요(49)

help 돕다(81)

hen 암탉(59)

hers 그녀의 것(14)

hide 숨기다, 숨다(81)

hill 언덕(80)

hit 때리다(81)

hold 잡다, 붙들다(11)

holiday 휴일, 공휴일(32)

home 집(6)

hope 바라다(45)

horse 말(39)

hospital 병원(16)

hot 더운, 뜨거운(115)

hotel 호텔(43)

hour 시간(63)

how 어떻게, 얼마나(49)

hungry 배고픈(15)

hurry 서두르다(82)

hurt 다치게 하다(82)

i

I 나는, 내가(11)

idea 생각(50)

if (만약)~라면(121)

in ~안에(101,121)

inside ~의 안쪽에(111)

island 섬(89)

it 그것은(45)

j

job 일, 직업(37)

Juice 주스(22)

jump 뛰어오르다(83)

jungle 밀림, 정글(89)

just 방금, 오직(117)

k

keep 계속하다(89)

kick 차다(89)

kill 죽이다, 없애다(83)

kind 친절한(91)

king 왕(89)

kitchen 부엌(6)

knee 무릎(11)

knife 칼(7)

knock 두드리다(83)

know 알다, 이해하다(83)

l

lady 숙녀, 부인(15)

lake 호수(70)

land 땅, 육지(70)

last 마지막으로(117)

late 늦은, 늦게 (94,104,107)

laugh 웃다(83)

leaf 나뭇잎(70)

learn 배우다(83)

left 왼쪽, 왼쪽의(115)

leg 다리(11)

lesson 수업(83)

let 시키다(83)

letter 편지(39)

library 도서관(83)

life 생명, 생활(39)

light(1) 가벼운(89)

light(2) 빛, 조명(89)

like 좋아하다(84)

lip 입술(12)

listen 듣다(50)

live 살다(39)

lonely 외로운(94)

long 긴(112)

look 보다(84)

lose 잃다(103)

loud 시끄러운(111)

love 사랑하다(84,105)

luck 행운(40)

lunch 점심(63)

m

man 남자(15)

mail 우편(40)

make 만들다(84)

map 지도(63)

market 시장(55)

marry 결혼하다(40)

matter 문제, 곤란(50)

may ~해도 좋다(84)

meat 고기(22)

meet 만나다(85)

mine 나의 것(15)

minute 분(63)

mirror 거울(7)

money 돈(55)

monkey 원숭이(89)

morning 아침(63)

mountain 산(70)

move 움직이다(85)

movie 영화(28)

music 음악(28)

must 꼭 해야만 한다(85)

n

near 가까운(99)

neck 목(12)

new 새로운(95)

next 다음의, 다음에(95)

nice 멋진(95)

night 밤(63)

noon 정오, 한 낮(64)

north 북쪽(64)

nose 코(12)

now 지금, 방금(117)

nurse 간호사(38)

o

office 사무실(16)

only 오직, 유일한(95)

open 열다(102)

out 밖으로, 밖에(101)

outside ~밖에(112)

q

question 질문(50)

quick 빠른(99)

quiet 조용한(96)

quiz 질문, 퀴즈(51)

p

pants 바지(25)

paper 종이(33)

parent 부모님(18)

party 파티, 모임(40)

pass 지나가다(85)

pay 지불하다(56)

peace 평화(40)

pear (과일)배(22)

people 사람들, 국민(15)

pick 따다(85)

picnic 소풍(46)

pig 돼지(60)

pilot 조종사(38)

pin 핀(33)

pink 분홍(36)

place 장소, 곳(46)

plant 식물(70)

play 연주하다, 놀다(86)

please 기쁘게 하다(86)

pocket 호주머니(25)

police 경찰(38)

pool 웅덩이, 연못(71)

poor 가난한(95,99)

pull 당기다(101)

push 밀다(101)

put 놓다, 두다(86)

r

rain 비, 비가오다(71)

rainbow 무지개(71)

read 읽다, 낭독하다(51)

ready 준비가 된(96)

record 기록하다(86)

red 빨간색, 붉은(36)

remember 기억하다(86)

restaurant 레스토랑(46)

rice 쌀, 밥(22)

rich 돈 많은(110)

right 오른쪽(114)

ride 타다(87)

ring(1) 반지(25)

ring(2) 울리다(87)

river 강(71)

road 길, 도로(46)

roof 지붕(7)

room 방(7)

round 둥근, 동그란(96)

run 달리다(87)

s

sad 슬픈(112,113)

safe 안전한(96)

salad 샐러드(22)

salt 소금(22)

same 동일한,똑같은(17,105)

sand 모래(71)

save 절약하다(114)

say 말하다(51)

school 학교, 수업(44)

sea 바다(72)

season 계절(64)

seat 자리, 좌석(17)

see 보다(87)

sell 팔다(109)

send 보내다(87)

shall ~일 것이다(88)

she 그녀는, 그녀가(16)

sheep 양(60)

ship 배(43)

shirt 셔츠(25)

shoe 신, 구두(26)

shoot 쏘다, 던지다(88)

shop 가게(56)

short 짧은(111,113)

shout 소리치다(88)

show 보이다(88)

shut 닫다, 덮다(102)

silent 조용한(111)

silver 은, 은빛, 은의(29)

sing 노래, 노래하다(29)

sit 앉다(101)

skate 스케이트(29)

skirt 스커트(26)

sled 썰매(29)

sleep 잠자다(14)

slide 미끄러지다(88)

slow 느린(96,113)

small 작은(94)

smart 영원한(110)

smell 냄새맡다(80)

smile 웃다, 미소지다(89)

snow 눈, 눈이오다(29)

soap 비누(7)

soccer 축구(29)

sofa 소파(6)

soft 부드러운(107)

son 아들(18)

song 노래(29)

soon 곧(118)

sorry 죄송한(97)

south 남쪽(64)

space 공간, 우주(29)

speak 말하다(51)

spell 철자(51)

spend 낭비하다(89)

spoon 숟가락, 스푼(8)

sport 스포츠(29)

spring 봄(64)

stair 계단(8)

star 별(29)

stand 서다,일어서다(101)

start 출발하다(100,101)

station 역, 정거장(17)

strawberry 딸기(23)

street 거리(47)

strike 때리다(89)

stop 멈추다(100)

store 가게, 상점(56)

story 이야기(52)

strong 힘이 센,강한(114)

student 학생(34)

study 공부하다(34)

stupid 어리석은(97)

subway 지하철(43)

summer 여름(65)

sun 태양, 햇빛(73)

supermarket 슈퍼마켓(56)

supper 저녁식사(23)

sweater 스웨터(26)

swim 수영하다, 수영(30)

swing 그네(30)

t

table 테이블(34)

take 받다(109)

talk 말하다(52)

tall 키가 큰(111)

taste 맛을 보다(89)

team 팀(30)

telephone 전화(8)

tell 말하다(52)

tennis 테니스(30)

test 시험, 검사(34)

thank 감사하다(97)

that 저것, 그것(16)

the 그(16)

then 그때, 그러면(118)

there 거기에(116)

they 그들은(16)

thick 두꺼운(98)

thin 얇은(98)

think ~라고 생각하다(52)

this 이것(17)

throw 던지다(90)

tie 넥타이(26)

tiger 호랑이(60)

today 오늘(65)

tomato 토마토(23)

tomorrow 내일(65)

tonight 오늘 밤(65)

tooth 이, 치아(12)

town 마을(41)

train 기차(43)

travel 여행, 여행하다(47)

trip 여행(47)

truck 트럭(43)

true 진실의(114)

u

ugly 못생긴,추한(103)

umbrella 우산(26)

v

very 매우, 아주(118)

video 비디오(30)

village 마을, 촌락(41)

visit 방문하다(65)

w

wait 기다리다(90)

walk 걷다, 산책하다(90)

waste 낭비하다(115)

water 물(73)

way 길, 방법(66)

we 우리, 저희가(17)

weak 약한(113)

week 주, 1주간(66)

welcome 환영하다(41)

well 만족하게, 잘(118)

west 서쪽(66)

wet 젖은, 축축한(97)

what 무엇, 어떤(52)

when 언제(53)

where 어디에(53)

which 어느쪽, 어느(53)

white 흰, 흰빛(36)

who 누구(53)

whom 누구를(53)

whose 누구의(54)

why 왜(54)

wind 바람(73)

window 창(창문)(8)

winter 겨울(66)

wood 나무, 숲(73)

word 낱말, 단어(54)

world 세계, 지구(73)

y

yellow 노랑(36)

yesterday 어제(66)

you 너, 당신(17)

yours 너의 것(17)

z

zoo 동물원(60)

초등 영단어 600 따라쓰기

재판 1쇄 발행 2019년 1월 10일

글 Y&M 어학 연구소

펴낸이 서영희 | **펴낸곳** 와이 앤 엠

편집 임명아 | **책임교정** 하연정

본문인쇄 명성 인쇄 | **제책** 정화 제책

제작 이윤식 | **마케팅** 강성태

주소 120-848 서울시 서대문구 홍은동 376-28

전화 (02)308-3891 | Fax (02)308-3892

E-mail yam3891@naver.com

등록 2007년 8월 29일 제312-2007-000040호

ISBN 978-89-93557-35-0 63740

본사는 출판물 윤리강령을 준수합니다.